For mother, father, and baby

I must leave
unfolded forever.

— Suji Kwock Kim

TABLE OF CONTENTS

I

II

III

IV

FOLDING A RIVER

poems

KAWITA KANDPAL

MARICK
PRESS

Library of Congress Cataloguing in Publication Data

Kandpal, Kawita
Folding A River.
Poems in English
ISBN 978-0-9712676-3-3

Copyright © Kawita Kandpal, 2006
Edited by Peter Markus
Design and typesetting by Sean Tai
Cover design by Sean Tai
Cover photography by Ian Tadashi Moore

Printed and bound in Canada

Marick Press
P.O. Box 36253
Grosse Pointe Farms
Michigan 48236
www.marickpress.com

Distributed by spdbooks.org

I

GRAVITY: THREE MOVEMENTS

It's the well of his palm she remembers. The ways sparrows nestle
     after the first snow on her window ledge. She shudders knowing
         how little
the human hand holds. Barely enough to carry water between rivers.
     Not enough for the sparrow's shadow she stoops for beside the yew.
She sings loss everyday with her body. She hummed it once
     after he made love to her. The sound she'll tell him years later
in a letter, after the loss of her only child, was the Ganges spilling
     out of her hand, a neglected sparrow's sigh.
And though a season of letters go unanswered,
     there is language in the silence she takes comfort in, memory
of bone between beautiful bone. It's like the first time
     sparrow wings fold, and his hands unfold across his face
when he hears a man and woman making love in the room next to his.
     It's the sparrow not knowing its song is complete, the bones sing
tra la la to the flesh, tra la la, tra la la, tra la la.

First Law Of Loss

Woman is the distance man invented,
the way one lets go of earthly delights.

And though the enlightened insist the gesture
gravity, it is the first law of loss in any language.

Consider Eve and DaVinci haunted by the heaviness of being
human. Knowledge evolved from lesser nouns, before we

Pronounced ourselves metaphor; curious bridge between what is
and what is supposed to be.

I have to believe our bodies occupy the sacred between sensual and semantics,
how beautifully it unfolds in another's hand, an apple blossom.

I imagine DaVinci's delight when he placed scalpel to skin and pressed a line
down the center; I wonder if he wondered what gardens awaited him within.

Some gestures stay with us, memory of a woman, first longing,
first love, call it what you will, it's what divides a darkened room in two.

And the body stretched across linen isn't you but the one you long to...
Oh, how delicious the descent, from heavenly body to heavenly body we fall.

Before Partition

Touch   what you can   not
                              see,

   Petals of light

Negotiate space   on pubis,

      First blossom   between her   parts:

There is no word   for the soft opening   of sky.

Dreaming, Kashmir

i.

There are words on your tongue I have considered embracing, a landscape
of water and stone. Yesterday, I dreamed of you in another language

and felt the vertigo of Kashmir, a singular gesture of not finding
my footing upon the edge of this page. As a scientist's daughter I have
    these notions

that gravity means more to the dead than the dying. What holds us here
is not the flesh, but the words beneath, when water was simply a sound.

ii.

What living does to the lesser is this: lends us luminous;
before ebbing into the far reaches of exotic, these echoes

of my Michigan exile call me back to the beginning of my home
land's original tongue.

iii.

I am falling inside the metaphor of another, a country
to call home. In your name, I have come to ask my ancestors, the word
       for *attachment* in Kashmiri. As you read the following,
my footpath will have already shifted

                to the other side of the mountain.

Mountain says to Sky: *myth is a vehicle of departure*
*from the weight of being huma*n.

iv.

     Today I learned there is no word for *human* in Kashmiri. It seems
          there is no place
in our language for failure. These margins of error are steep enough for
     the light falling
          from a woman's face after a man lends a thousand sadnesses
to her. In dreams, the gesture is returned as a calligraphy of cranes.

v.

          I long to believe being human holds more than the potential
of taking flight from another's hand. I know a man near the coast
     who translates the gravity of loss between white space. I have drawn
     the distance
of his name as a line of birds, lifting
               from these words.

WHAT BREAKS US

Crush my eyes, bitter grapes:
wring out the wine of seeing.
   — Suji Kwock Kim

He made a lovely light
on shores opposite the ebb of his eyes.

Consider the horizon line reflected in the iris,
Laguna Veneta, I, too, am separated by such desires.

Sweet Veneta, how do you surrender a purposeful hue the shape of Murano
swirls? The water of every woman's center is his

second city of glass. Once I wished to appear within
the abbreviated range of his sight. I could go on and on,

a century of artisans rendered *objects d'art* with breath, could blow
hollow a civilization. My dearest, the ghost of what was once,

still is, a form of abandon, the artisans abrupt shift to the bluer edge
of another Eden, like the bead of islands bearing a deeper shade of sorrow

upon your iris. I have to look away from the proof
of our existence. This vision remains: you are an angel

separated from your own light, outlined by the recurring theme
that what breaks us is at the surface. Even now, these words

are floating towards deeper translation, and I am collecting our days before the sentences fold close, between darkness and darkness.

Blueprints Of The Universe

Our fingers, half-crescents of light,
can fold prayers into eyelids.

Your skin, the history of evening sky, I have printed
a narrative of days for you. Here,

my name, a constellation of kisses,
connects the darkness of two.

Surviving Eden: Field Notes

Call it a ceremony of praise,
cathedrals of poplars lean into prairie grass
this side of solitude.

Countryside of my longest lonely,
how I praise your gestures of resilience.
White willows inspire on lesser days.

Once my father showed me how to fold our back field of winter wheat
in my palms, like prayer. From his sick bed, he folded my hands in his,
two snowy egrets, netted in a death song.

At winter's end, I return to the place of wheat and willows,
and my father, how I praise what endures;
the soft green emerges and the weeping willow still weeps
each impossible season.

VEIL

Dear father,   I wear   your absence

    in my eyes;   my fiancé   left a fortnight   after   I refused

his hands,   incapable of sharing,   I can not bear   skin

    inside skin;   history holds   a deeper *escarus*,   the weight

I want utterly;   to wear   instead   this veil.

TRANSLATION

Some days I hear your voice
calling *Lola* through this house,

as it settles further into the ground, closer
to the soil that is slowly erasing your mouth.

You come to me then
through the bamboo floors

that speak in syncopated code,
a dead father to his daughter.

These moments when you speak
are measured through the force of my footsteps

that ache to translate the hollow sounds
of your voice knotted in wood,

this yearning to press closer to your mouth,
like a kiss, or a tear.

Some days I wait in the evenings,
press my fingertips to open holes in the wood,

speaking with my hands,
spelling my name on your lips.

WEIGHT, MEMORY

Father taught me the alphabet
when I was one, rearranging constellations,

spelling *daughter* in evening sky. *Hold this,* he said,
and gave me a handful of water chestnuts.

I labored under the weight of the gift, miniature moons
which proved a heavier lesson than their sweetness.

SWEETNESS

To behold an orange promises an orchard
all year long.

Its soft covering falls
in two scented hemispheres.

This round jubilance keeps its contents
of ocean and tide quiet, still.

Once, my uncle wrestled free an infant's brain
that resisted separation during autopsy.

I was there to record organ weights. It took two men,
four hands, *stubborn son of a bitch*, they agreed,

peeling back a continent of bone;
the idiot thing was still smiling

when they dropped the halves
on the scale. I want to weigh memory in my palms

like a crate of clementines. Nature remembers itself
through sweetness, the repetition of orchards that bring themselves back

from season to succulent season; there are moments
not meant to be remembered: some minds

are too small to carry
the sweetness of this world.

ANY LANDSCAPE, ANY LOSS

Consider the blossom: impossibly small. The smallest gesture
of hope outlived only by winter. I, too, am becoming
a little less than my namesake. I am conscious of the exhale,

and what it takes with it. Thief of good fortune, the dead are among us.
Winter interrupts even them. I can feel the half close
of memory. I am already yesterday to this passing season.

All that I still love falls away like kisses;
my lover's curved torso in the bath,
Genevieve the cat tracing the barn's shadow,

my breasts pressed against the bedroom door frame during love.
I am between the country of coming and going
of this door's momentum. And so we are, ourselves, becoming elegy.

This time next year you will have evolved into an idea. In Hindi,
I learned every sadness has a name: a hard ceremony of loss.
These are the two things I wish to remember about love and what it does

to us. Flesh is first to forget the ceremony of body:
this is the agreement at birth. We leave earth's dark embrace with less
than what we came with. What remains: perhaps the blossom of a woman's hips
in spring, there is little else for the asking.

Once after love, you asked me if I believed in life after life. I cannot say I know
even now, each day gifted with something that unfolds slowly within.
This much is true: our bodies are lit by the moon, and one evening you shall

return from the barn heavy with the fields to find me
seamless in sleep. I am lining all our wine glasses on the sill,
watching you turn the soil down like prayer.

Each day we part, the distance grows less interrupted.
Love, some days I cannot bear the wait and wish of sky.
I want to ease into the infinite, believe at a certain hour my words will
soften bone to *white* to *winter* to *stars*.

Longing Can Be That Heavy, That Holy

The Ganges is drunk again,
        its stupor as long as a woman's
sadness. In dreams, I am that woman
        who embraces the darker currents
of her history, this holy water
        between my legs.
The Ganges Plain drinks all rivers,
        making water a memory for the living.
Desert can make the human body
        forget love. Bone forgets body
to merge with myth downstream.
        There must be more to dreams than this
burning desert, save rivers of ash.
        I have to believe there are continents submerged
in centuries of desire.
        Still, there is the history of water,
if only in sleep.

Language Of Lakes

We were both leaving landscapes:
            him a marriage, me the Midwest.

Neither of us seeking tenderness
      elusive as fingerprints on water.

It's the memory of water that stays
                  long after the virgin pines have ebbed
                        into a naturalist's sketchbook of the Great Lakes.

How I envy water, no history of the hand.
      I wonder if sorrow also shaped the trinity
            of inland seas. If I awoke early in the day would Superior remember
                  how much loss she holds —

And so it is, he and I emerged,
            from a decade of losing ground
                  longing for more than the language of lakes.

At the edge of my Michigan lonely
      I trace Huron and Erie in dreams,
            a canoe following the crease of shore.

And him, waist high in the current,
            lifting impressions of water on his pencil,
                  drawing me home.

JADE

Here is the delicate jade,
a strand of snow peas
between mother's breasts.
    Though her fingers could coax
Himalayan snow into pearls,
she preferred jade;
    a river that encircled her neck,
a gift bridge from father
when he pulled his beloved towards him,
    once so hard jade spilled
between floorboards; the cold green melting
in its own sweet light.

NULLIPARA

After cremation the men lifted your bones, alabaster
       skull like the half moon rising outside
              the hospital window the night you died.

Ash is what remains after your fifty-two years.
       There is barely enough to fill this vessel, as you have
           filled my life, and now my lap. You carried me

for two decades, like a mother who refused
       to give birth. I will deliver you to the Ganges
         where our ancestors await you

and me one day. Remembering the man
      who collected your bones saying,
          well, would you look at this, a damn near whole set of teeth.

         He held it up above his head,
            to toast me a longer life.

Apologia

Until the banyan leaves push *yes* in spring, I will carry us.
We embrace the same water and all the words that go with it.

Little one, we grow into two landscapes,
and all I can do is cradle you in your dark lullaby of days.

ONCE

Praise
      the phalaenopsis,
bent with 18th century
      melancholia,
outlined in resplendent
      ivory: winter's bride.

Oh, sweet ebb
      of empire,
how you elongate the silhouette
      of longing; a measured seduction
of light and loss, an Andalusian sadness
      patinas your petals
sepia, ever softly.

Sweet phalaenopsis, I wish to be
      your still life; companion
in solitude, one
      whose stubborn refusal of seasons
lends this hour gravity, grace.

GHOSTS

The Ojibwa have a word for absence:
I forget. They lived on the plains
of northern Michigan, brown clouds that bled
when you pierced the soft underbelly.

I know you know. Try the weight of the north
in your palms. History is as heavy as any animal
this side of myth. Imagine steam locomotives halting
to allow a herd of clouds to pass over.

The landscape always remembers and so do the songs
of the Ojibwa. They sing absence through a bison horn,
call back clouds from their westward migration,

corral ghosts into a circle of water. Sieve the heaviest
tears into a river that separates prairie
from sky; hooves will fall so softly.

Red Sea

There is a vein   in everything

        see   how a single tributary   of desire

            pulses   towards divine.

DIVINE, WORK

You articulate desire by the number of days
      to arrive at a poem on the other side of the river Rouge.

Four tributaries, less than a hand contains as many vices
      as the barons who shaped the skyline one brick at a breath.

Smokestacks held count of the hands who passed through
      the doors of Highland Park, emerging darker, more perfect

Angels upon a fresco across the city in the Church of St. Paul on Woodward;
    there is
      divine in the gestures of those who work with their hands.

The sounds of work have many tools; the man who blind rivets metal
      to metal is one, the man who presses lips upon angel wings is the
      other.

WHO HOLDS MORE LIGHT

Collapse the word   father   into figure   of a ghost,

    one who holds more light   in absence;   how is it   an outline can

accommodate the dead   and not the dying? I wish to wear   the halo

    of melancholy   that was the cloth   you left us;

I collect your memory   of pressed suits   in steamer trunks,

    folding less   your stooped frame   haunting my doorway.

I hear you,   father,   some evenings   half moons of ice

    in a hand rendered scotch glass,   the only language   we speak.

LANGUAGE OF BONE

Even the ocean, submerged in the deserts
of the Ganges Plain, found its origins deep

in a chapter of sediments. Every narrative begins
with water, birth of diaphanous blue,

its pages unfolding into centuries of desire.
Even before the Kama Sutra,

lullabies translated longing into historical cities
with names like Kandahar, Varanasi, and Allahabad.

Before language, there was the long bone,
because it held human memory longest.

Edge Of Sweetwater Seas

The waves fold my sorrow
        into a wing, a wish,
words lend water the shape of narrative. My father's
hand arcs a flight path upon the page.
        He, the crane; I, the reed
ebbing into blue.

DRINK

Here,   hold this   blunt edge   of evening

    sky;   my dearest,   we fold   moments

in half,   our words   scissor cumulous

    into snowflakes   falling, I   am curving

towards desire;   your mouth   a cup.

Float, Memory

Hands float memory   of days;   sky

    the shape of longing,   sorrow

Minus its reflection   confirms both sides are

    still   petals apart   from the Sweetwater seas;

My hands lift   daughter's face   in dreams,

    come evening,   scent of lily   brings her near   my name.

Folding a River

for P

Begin with the current and fold once,
in the direction of travel, to minimize splashing.

Do not despair. Continue to fold blue upon blue until a wing emerges
in the shape of a crane.

Cradle gently. Place under tongue, and release,
not letting prayer fall from your lips.

AFTER PARTITION

Father, you touched a girl into woman   and I am still less

                                             woman.

     Reconciliation is the country   we can (hope)   not share. In dreams

You are still   amongst the dead.

CROSSING THE INTERIOR

Consider the trespass   of breath,

        Our bodies of light   are ghosts

In outline.   We carry   the absence   within

       White space;   between semantics we exhale,   the dead

Interrupt   sans apology.   Father

       Why do you travel   evenings   to trace my exile?

FUCK

is the word
    in the wound;
one cannot soften
    verb with father's hand,
I have attempted
    a return to Eden before
language failed; my tongue
    the last petal blushed with light
carries the gesture home.

Giambattista Tiepolo's Christ Calming The Storm

Is this the man?
By him who died on cross,
With his cruel bow he laid full low
The harmless Albatross.
— Samuel Taylor Coleridge, *Rime of the Ancient Mariner*

It wasn't the blue squall between sea and sky
        on canvas by Tiepolo's trident that made me look.

It wasn't even Christ, whose arms were thrust upwards
        against the gale forces, a tarp above the squatting men
            in the brown reed boat.

It was, indeed, a black crescent in the clouds overhead
        that cycloned off the canvas.

It might have been a mark I would have made
        by accident; dabbing black onto my brush
            and arcing it across an expanse of cloud
                in the corner of the sea's storm.

Maybe it was the way Tiepolo would have wanted
        it, an imperfect signature in oil. A good omen
            like Coleridge's Albatross.

I wanted to lift blackness up off the clouds,
        not like the ancient mariner,
            who rendered the bird flightless
              with a crossbow.

I wanted to believe I could nest a shadow
     in my palm and possess feathers.
          Christ's body and the ship's hull bowed
              under the weight of the storm.

His blue robe flapping like the boat's sail.
     The cloth always assumes more
          than it can contain. The second skin
              that covers the body is not enough
                  to sustain a body upright.

Christ buoys, ankle deep in blue tide.
     I smudged the stain, instead, into more storm
          clouds. Only the mariner would know
              I failed to lift a shadow from the sky,
                silencing the bird's body
                    into a black static blur.

I removed the carcass from the canvas,
     feathered flakes of dried pigment
          and hung it upon my neck
              with a single sweeping stroke of my finger,

like the necklace that replaced
     the mariner's cross before the bird fell
     into the sea.

There was a tear where that portion of sky was.
     Stigmata in blue veined flesh. The waves
          curling higher off the canvas, the tear bleeding
              black into lesser forms of being.

Eulogy Of Trees

How to collect words from ghosts, father,
I revisit the passage of our last year with your pen

Envying the lesson of apple trees, letting go of the gone;
in increments, I too am learning how

This ledger of days subtracts seasons
like the orchard framed in the garden pond.

GROUNDED

I've watched you uncomfortable beneath goose down
clouds. They weigh heavy with your perspiration.
Feather quills pinch and poke out a quilted cave
to outline your form. These feathers feel like tumors
they found bristling inside your liver, you say.

I offer you food and drink, distraction to push you up
into another day's sunrise. My mouth presses words
like marriage and future grandchildren into your cheek.
You want me to take down the hanging bird feeder
outside the bedroom window. Those birds split seed, squawk,

scatter. This talk of feathers and nests has made you tired.
Some have even tried to fly in, mistaking the window
for sky. At evening's end, I help you lift
your arms upward and downward

to keep muscles from stiffening. It is then you refuse
to look at the moon. You say your body will become that
stone which swells and stiffens in the night sky.
I want to tell you that these hands of mine
will roll back stones from your cave;
your body will rise without feathers.

OPEN, SEASON
for V

This was not the way I wrote the hour of our name,
the one that means absence of desire. Happiness

flickered in the window's reflection, the face of diminishing returns.
The one who calculates the rate of snowflakes falling outside the song

of lost peacocks. We can open this season like a song bird,
and follow the sound of blue to the origins of discontent, an approximate end

to every flame inside the living word. I want more than the arc of departure
        between days,
the rib's curve suggests point B lends point A greater purpose,

non-linear, a delicate aria any woman would envy.
Grace divines the shape of an open season, a semi-circular splendor

of plumes. Within a book of Persian blues a jeweled sky
can be undone by a single breath.

From beyond the late day of ones namesake, in the rising
hour, a narrative of evening sky unfolds a crescent moon

in the likeness of a woman's profile,
her gesture of eyelids carry the landscape of sleep, a place to call home.

FORGIVEN

When I came to know that elephants mourn
the passing of their own, keep a vigil
only they can know, I understood forgiveness
and how it comes disguised as soil,
a solitary place, respite for the dead
traveler. And though we can't take credit
for natural death, this land has final claims
on all flesh. Without hesitation it takes back a life
summarized by blood and bone as if to say, *I've lent you
a part of me, and now I've come for it.* The dark

color of soil also lends some men their demeanor,
especially those with hands that know no tenderness,
only black beneath. I once saw a man
bring down a mother elephant, two babies at her side. It didn't take a lot
to know they'd be orphaned standing beside the massive body, still
breathing, the herd moving on to the next watering hole.
It's too easy to assume death comes only to the slow and stupid, one man
who keeps just the feet needing wastebaskets for his country home.

I don't always understand forgiveness,
and I wonder if the earth doesn't either, sometimes refusing
to take back a man's body, leaving it
for the truly hungry who roam the darkened land
alone. Would it say, *I've lent you nothing,
you have no part of me I wish for.* It's likely earth would
first remove harshness from the human
hand, render bone soft as sponge.
Groundwater will make a river out of the ribs

on which a heart will drift. And so the land continues
to keep claims to itself, tenderly
taking back the mistakes of men.

GRAVITY OF DAYS

Heart is the darkest corner of night,
desire the shape of a woman, a man.

Behind rice paper screens
two shadows touch and part.

Oh, the ancient sorrows of longing
in Basho's book of days.

Her heart was the night blooming jasmine.
His, the shadow of the tree.

In Basho's book of days it is written desire has three names:
absence, longing, grace.

What he calls lonely, she calls longing.
Bed linens recall the curve of her breast,

the small of his back. In dreams, they can touch
hollows of despair.

In Basho's book of days it is also written, *solitude is the country
between the living and the non-living.*

Even the jasmine, burdened with the weight of sweetness,
lets go of summer in a shiver of petals.

In letters, he writes, fireflies are half night sky, half light.
In letters, she writes, the gravity of days bend, break.

Acknowledgements

The author gratefully acknowledges:

Susan Hahn at *TriQuarterly*
Kathleene West at *Puerto del Sol*
Cheri L.R. Roberts
Robert Fanning
Vievee Francis-Olzmann

Thank you too to:

Patti Abbott, Ron Allen, Anthony Ambrogio, Olivia V. Ambrogio, Vijayant Bhatt, Anthony Butts, Carol Campell, Claire Crabtree, Debby and Rick Davies, Irene Finnegan, John Gallagher, Perri Giovannuci, Ann Green, Mariela Griffor, Marijo Grogan, James E. Hart III, Lolita Hernandez, Lonnie Hull Dupont, Kelly Inman, Beverly Istvan, Mary Chi-Whi Kim, Jean Lantis, Patrick O'Leary, Greg Mans, Jeff Mans, Ted Miller, Ian Tadashi Moore, Matthew Scott Olzmann, Maria Orlowski, Milton and Margaret Porter, Mary Beth Reasoner, John Rybicki, Suzanne Scarfone, Jane Schaberg, Nicole Schuster, Mamta Sharma, Peggy Stack, Ste. Anne de Detroit, Robert Sterner, Anne Stewart, Robert Taylor, Russell Thorburn, J. Harlan Underhill, Anca Vlasopolos, Rayfield A. Waller, Ron and Carol Wisner, Martha Bell Wright, and my beautiful family.

Peter Markus, you are luminous. I am blessed to call you brother.

I am most grateful to my mother and father who taught me to love in two languages.

MEMBER OF SCABRINI GROUP

Québec, Canada
2007